George Washington

Written by:
Lori Kaiser

Illustrated by:
Lori Kaiser and Colton Kaiser

Published by Carpe Diem Publishers
17401 Betty Blvd.
Canyon, TX 79015
806-433-6321

www.carpediempublishers.com

© Copyright, 2012 by Carpe Diem Publishers. All Rights Reserved. No portion of this book may be reproduced, stored in a retrieval system, or transmitted, in any form or by any means, electronic, mechanical, photocopying, recording, or otherwise without prior written permission from publisher.
Printed in the United States of America
ISBN 978-0-9836651-7-5

Dedicated to my friend, and fellow-author, Lesa Boutin, who encouraged me to pursue my writing. Thank you for all your help!

The father of our country is well known and very loved.

Washington was a man who depended on his faith.

He would look to God for help
in decisions that he made.

Wearied of the politics
and feeling rather old,

Facts About George Washington

Birthday:
February 22, 1732, in Pope's Creek, VA

Died:
December 14, 1799, in Mount Vernon, VA, at 67 years old.

Age at Inauguration:
57 years old

Political Party:
Federalist

Terms in Office:
Two. (April 30, 1789 - March 3, 1797)

Vice President:
John Adams

First Lady:
Martha Dandridge Custis Washington

Children:
None of his own. He had two stepchildren.

Illustrations

Some illustrations in this book are the illustrator's drawings of National Archive pictures.

References

National Geographic's "Our Country's Presidents"

www.ingramcontent.com/pod-product-compliance
Lightning Source LLC
Chambersburg PA
CBHW042046290426
44109CB00001B/45